SPORTSMATH

HOW IT WORKS

SPORTSMATH

HOW IT WORKS

Lee Arthur/Elizabeth James/Judith B. Taylor

Lothrop, Lee & Shepard Company
A Division of William Morrow & Company, Inc.

New York

For Jason,
Jeff and Steve,
Amy and Stephen

Library of Congress Cataloging in Publication Data

Arthur, Lee (date)
    Sportsmath: how it works.

    SUMMARY: Demonstrates how basic math is used to find averages, percentages, projections, and other calculations in football, baseball, basketball, hockey, and tennis by describing one important actual game in each sport.
    1. Sports—Statistics—Juvenile literature.
2. Arithmetic—1961-   —Juvenile literature.
[1. Sports—Statistics. 2. Arithmetic] I. James,
Elizabeth, joint author. II. Taylor, Judith B.,
joint author. III. Title.
GV741.A75   796   75–17714
ISBN 0–688–41712–4
ISBN 0–688–51712–9 lib. bdg.

ACKNOWLEDGMENTS

The authors wish to thank Carol and Chris Szulc, Norma Daly, June MacDonald, John Rudzik, and Mike Taylor, who contributed their assistance and support in the writing of this book. We also wish to thank Carol Barkin, whose creative editing and confidence in the book helped make it a reality.

Many thanks also to the following organizations and individuals for their generous help in answering questions and providing official information: the National Football League, especially Don Weiss; the Baltimore Colts; the New York Jets; the American and National Leagues, especially Marty Appel of the New York Yankees; the Executive Offices of the National Basketball Association; the National Hockey League, especially Robert Casey; the U.S. Lawn Tennis Association, especially Stan Malless, Mike Burns, and Pret Hadley.

CONTENTS

INTRODUCTION

Have you ever noticed how many numbers there are in sports? Not just scores, but batting averages, shooting percentages, passing yardages, or minutes remaining in a game?

When you listen to a game on the radio or watch one on television, the sportscaster uses a lot of numbers or statistics to give you more information about the game. During a football game, for instance, the announcer tells you how many yards are gained or lost on each play as it happens. In a basketball game, the announcer keeps track of the score, and also gives you information about the shooting percentage of each team and of individual players. At the end of any kind of game or during time-outs or halftime, the sportscaster tells you all the important statistics of the game. You might call these figures "sportsmath."

Usually the sportscaster doesn't have time to do all this math —he or she is too busy watching the action and giving a play-by-play account of what's happening. The job of doing sportsmath goes to the game statistician, who sits in the announcer's booth and keeps track of all the important numbers on game charts. The statistician does whatever math is needed so the sportscaster can keep you up to date on the statistics. Copies of all these figures often go to newspaper reporters at the end of the game to help them write their articles.

Sportsmath really isn't anything more than basic arithmetic— adding and subtracting, multiplying and dividing. The action of each game, for instance, may involve both adding up scores and subtracting minutes played to see how much time is left. Overall statistics for a completed game are mainly averages and percentages, and these are all done by division. This means that most sportsmath is really long division.

But sportsmath statistics are constantly changing. A player's or team's performance in each game is combined with the statistics from previous games to find the overall season performance, and of course this keeps on changing right up to the end of each season. So the statistics published in one day's newspaper won't be up to date the next day, if another game was played in the meantime.

This book describes one big game in each of five sports— football, baseball, basketball, hockey, and tennis. After you have gone through the games in the book and worked the sportsmath problems for each one, you'll be able to keep track of the changing fortunes of your favorite teams and players by doing sportsmath on your own. As you watch or listen to a game, use paper and pencil to figure out what's happening. Then you'll have up-to-the-minute information, without waiting for the next day's papers.

You may even want to make your own charts like the ones the game statisticians use—the charts often make it easier to jot down all the different numbers you want to know. This book shows you what the charts look like, as well as explaining how to use the numbers to do sportsmath.

FOOTBALL SPORTSMATH

Some people think that football has moved ahead of baseball as the most popular spectator sport in the U.S. And many people think it's the most complicated sport in terms of numbers. In each game, besides the score, you have to keep track of first downs, yardage gained, yards needed for a first down, and minutes remaining in the game. That may seem like plenty of sportsmath.

But for the players and for the overall standings, averages are just about the most important kind of football sportsmath. Average yards gained per pass, average yards gained per rushing attempt, average yards per punt or per offensive play—all of these are used to find out who are the record holders and the best players in each category every season.

To find these averages, you have to divide the total number of yards by the number of attempts or plays. If a player gained 10 yards in 5 rushing attempts, his average would be 10 divided by 5, or 2 yards per rushing attempt: $10 \div 5 = 2$.

Using the facts of football, you can figure out the important averages for the third Super Bowl game, played in January, 1969.

Football Facts

Time: 4 quarters, 15 minutes playing time each
Field: 160 feet wide, 100 yards long; goal posts 23 feet 4 inches apart
Scoring: touchdown, 6 points;

FOOTBALL FIELD

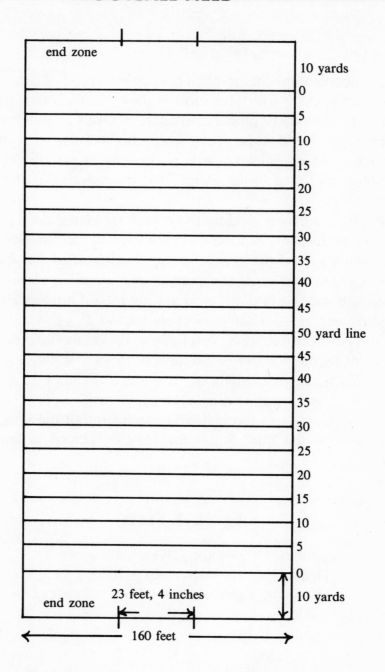

end zone

10 yards

0

5

10

15

20

25

30

35

40

45

50 yard line

45

40

35

30

25

20

15

10

5

0

10 yards

23 feet, 4 inches

end zone

160 feet

extra point after touchdown, 1 point;
field goal, 3 points;
safety, 2 points

Play: To keep possession of the ball, a team gets 4 tries (downs) to move the ball at least 10 yards toward the other team's goal. After the ball is moved 10 yards or more, another set of 4 downs begins with a first down.

Number of players: 11 on each team on the field at one time

Rosters for Super Bowl III

Jets

Offense

Sauer (end)
Hill (left tackle)
Talamini (left guard)
Schmitt (center)
Rasmussen (right guard)
Herman (right tackle)
Lammons (tight end)
Namath (quarterback)
Maynard (flanker)
Boozer (running back)
Snell (running back)
Turner (kicker)

Defense

Philbin (left end)
Rochester (left tackle)
Elliott (right tackle)
Biggs (right end)
Baker (left linebacker)
Atkinson (middle linebacker)
Grantham (right linebacker)
Sample (left halfback)
Beverly (right halfback)
Hudson (left safety)
Baird (right safety)

Substitutions

Mathis, Richardson, D'Amato, Johnson, Rademacher, Richards, Dockery, Smolinski, Crane, Neidert, Walton, Parilli, McAdams, J. Turner, Baird

Did not play

Christy, Gordon, Thompson

13

Colts

Offense

Orr (end)
Vogel (left tackle)
Ressler (left guard)
Curry (center)
Sullivan (right guard)
Ball (right tackle)
Mackey (tight end)
Morrall (quarterback)
Richardson (flanker)
Matte (running back)
Hill (running back)
Michaels (kicker)

Defense

Bubba Smith (left end)
B.R. Smith (left tackle)
Miller (right tackle)
Braase (right end)
Curtis (left linebacker)
Gaubatz (middle linebacker)
Shinnick (right linebacker)
Boyd (left halfback)
Lyles (right halfback)
Logan (left safety)
Volk (right safety)

Substitutions

J. Williams, Mitchell, Austin, Hawkins, Perkins, Cole, Szymanski, Porter, Hilton, Lee, Brown, Pearson, Dukes, Johnson, S. Williams, Unitas

Did not play

Ward

Super Bowl III

Few football games have ever been as dramatic as the third Super Bowl between the New York Jets and the Baltimore Colts in January of 1969.

It wasn't supposed to be an exciting game. The Jets represented the American Football League, which was considered much inferior to the longer established National Football League. And the first two Super Bowls had done nothing to change the AFL's image. The Green Bay Packers of the NFL had won easily in both 1967 and 1968, and the Colts were favored to beat the Jets in the third Super Bowl by a wide margin.

Jets' quarterback Joe Namath calling signals during Super Bowl III.
United Press International Photo

But brash Joe Namath, the Jets' young, highly paid quarterback, showed his usual flair for making headlines. He amazed the sports world before the game by boldly "guaranteeing" a Jets victory.

Namath had made a lot of enemies in the football world with his constant showing off, his long hair and mustache, and his loudmouthed bragging about himself and his team. So while the New York fans were hoping for a Jets victory, a lot of other people were hoping to see "Broadway Joe" take a fall.

By looking at some pre-game statistics, you can figure out the averages for some of the Colts and Jets players as they went into the Super Bowl. This will give you a way of comparing the teams and figuring out who was likely to win.

Sportscasters and reporters use several kinds of charts to keep track of the action as a game is played. The following charts show passing, rushing, and kicking averages for various players; you can make your own charts like these and fill in the players' names and their averages as you work them out. You might also make charts to use the next time you watch a football game.

PASSING

Baltimore	passing attempts	yards gained	average	New York	passing attempts	yards gained	average
MORRALL 1968 season	317	2909		NAMATH 1968 season	380	3147	
first half of Super Bowl				first half of Super Bowl			
Super Bowl total				Super Bowl total			

16

1. The passing chart shows Morrall's and Namath's number of passing attempts and their total yards gained for the 1968 season. From these figures you can work out their average yards gained per pass. Note that these averages for quarterbacks are based on the number of passes that were attempted, not on the number of passes that were completed.

Strategy: To find this kind of average, divide the number of yards gained by the number of passing attempts. Put a decimal point and two zeroes after the number of yards before dividing; you will work out your answer to two decimal places and then round it to the nearest tenth.

For Morrall, the problem would look like this: $2909.00 \div 317 = 9.17$. Rounding to the nearest tenth gives an average of 9.2 yards per attempted pass for Morrall's 1968 season.

Now figure out Namath's 1968 average the same way, and enter both players' averages in your chart.

2. Using the rushing chart on page 18, you can work out the average yards per carry for each running back (a carry is a rushing attempt). Then you can make another comparison between the two teams' performance in the 1968 season.

Strategy: To find the average yards gained per carry, divide the number of yards by the number of carries. For Hill's average, the problem would look like this: $360.00 \div 91 = 3.95$. Again, work the problem to two decimal places and round your answer to the nearest tenth. Rounding off Hill's average gives 4.0 average yards per carry.

Do the same for the other three running backs and enter the averages in your chart.

3. You can also figure out the average yards per field goal attempt for the kickers on the two teams during the 1968 season (see the chart on page 18).

Strategy: Divide the number of yards made by the number of field goals attempted for each kicker to find the averages.

RUSHING

Baltimore	carries	yards gained	average	New York	carries	yards gained	average
HILL				SNELL			
1968 season	91	360		1968 season	179	747	
first half of Super Bowl				first half of Super Bowl			
Super Bowl total				Super Bowl total			
MATTE				BOOZER			
1968 season	183	662		1968 season	143	441	
first half of Super Bowl				first half of Super Bowl			
Super Bowl total				Super Bowl total			

KICKING, 1968 SEASON

Baltimore	field goals attempted	total yards made	New York	field goals attempted	total yards made
Michaels	28	436	Turner	46	897

You can see from the averages you have found that Baltimore had a slightly better record in everything but field goals for the 1968 season. In addition, Morrall was considered a more reliable quarterback than Namath. These are some of the reasons why Baltimore was favored to win the Super Bowl. A crowd of 75,377 turned out at the Orange Bowl in Miami; millions more watched the game on television; and most of these people believed that they were about to see Joe Namath go down to defeat.

The Colts kicked off, but the Jets were unable to bring the ball across the 50-yard line before losing it. Johnson punted for the Jets, and the Colts received on their own 18-yard line. They carried the ball to the Jets' 27-yard line, but then Lou Michaels missed a field goal attempt. Surprisingly, the Jets had the ball again in a scoreless game.

Neither team managed to score for the whole first quarter. But Namath completed a few passes, and Snell, the Jets' big running back, gained 19 yards in the quarter. It began to look as if the Colts might have a tough afternoon.

The Jets made the game's first score in the second quarter when Snell ran around the left side from the 4-yard line for a touchdown. Turner made the point after touchdown, and it was 7–0 Jets.

New York fans were delighted to see the Jets go ahead of Baltimore; but most people still believed that Earl Morrall would lead the Colts to victory in the end.

Morrall had been with the Colts for only one year; he had been acquired as back-up quarterback for the ailing Johnny Unitas. Morrall had been named the NFL's Most Valuable Player for 1968. Before the Super Bowl he had said that it would be easy to throw short passes against the Jets, because their linebackers had been leaving a lot of room. Morrall had also predicted that the Colts would win the game by 18 points. At halftime, however, the Jets still led 7–0.

During halftime activities, the reporters and game statisticians were busy figuring out the statistics for the first half.

19

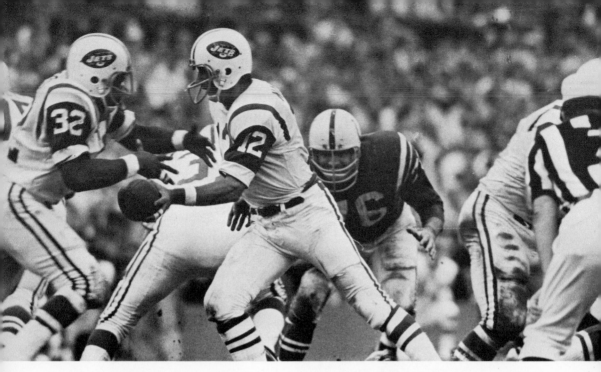

Quarterback Namath (number 12) hands off the ball to running back Emerson Boozer (number 32) during Super Bowl III.

United Press International Photo

For the running backs on both teams, the individual statistics looked like this at the half:

RUSHING, FIRST HALF OF SUPER BOWL

New York	carries	yards gained	Baltimore	carries	yards gained
Boozer	3	−1	Matte	5	76
Snell	16	71	Hill	7	16

4. Figure out the halftime rushing averages (average yards gained per carry) for the running backs.

Strategy: To find an average, remember that you must divide the total number of yards by the number of carries. Since Boozer did not gain any yards—in fact, he lost 1 yard—his average will be less than zero: $-1.00 \div 3 = -.33$ or $-.3$ yards per carry. Since Boozer was the only running back who lost yardage in the first half, his average is the only one that will be a negative number (less than zero).

You can work out the other three running backs' averages yourself. Work each answer to two decimal places and round to the nearest tenth. Then enter these averages in your overall rushing chart.

5. How were the two quarterbacks doing at the half? Here are the figures:

PASSING, FIRST HALF OF SUPER BOWL

New York	passing attempts	yards gained	Baltimore	passing attempts	yards gained
Namath	16	111	Morrall	15	71

Find the average yards gained per passing attempt for each quarterback.

Strategy: Divide the number of yards gained by the number of passing attempts. Again, work your answer to two decimal places and then round it to the nearest tenth.

These averages can now be entered in your chart; they give you one way of comparing the two quarterbacks' performances in the first half.

6. When they began their touchdown drive, the Jets had the ball on their own 20-yard line. Twelve plays later they scored. What was their average gain per play for this drive?

21

Strategy: First you have to figure out how many yards the touchdown drive covered. Since the Jets started on their own 20-yard line, subtract 20 from 100 (the length of the whole field) to find the yardage they covered.

Then divide the number of yards covered by the number of plays to find the average yardage per play.

As the second half got under way, the Jets got the ball on a Baltimore fumble. Almost 5 minutes into the third quarter, Turner kicked a 32-yard field goal and the score was 10–0 Jets.

The Colts seemed unable to move the ball. After losing 2 yards in three plays, they punted and the Jets had the ball again. After 11 minutes and 2 seconds of the third quarter, Turner kicked another field goal 30 yards to make it 13–0 for the Jets.

Now the Colts were definitely in trouble—not only were the Jets leading, but they showed no signs of slowing down. To spark the Colts back to life, injured veteran star Johnny Unitas was brought in to replace Morrall. Colts fans were sure this move would turn the game around—they thought the old pro, even with an injury, would lead his team to triumph.

Unitas made a tremendous effort, throwing almost as many passes in the short time he played as Namath threw in the entire game. But luck seemed to be against the Colts. Just over a minute and a half into the fourth quarter, Turner added three more points with a 9-yard field goal. On Baltimore's next drive Unitas's pass into the end zone was intercepted by the Jets' Beverly. Finally, with 3:19 to go in the game, the Colts scored their single touchdown, a 1-yard run by Jerry Hill. But it was clear that Baltimore wouldn't be able to catch up. When the final gun sounded, the Jets had won it, 16–7, in one of the most astonishing and historic upsets in the history of professional football.

After the reporters had recovered from their surprise, they

were anxious to see the game totals. The numbers were bound to be interesting for this first AFL win at the Super Bowl. Here are some of the figures:

RUSHING, SUPER BOWL TOTALS

New York	carries	yards gained	Baltimore	carries	yards gained
Boozer	10	19	Morrall	2	−2
Snell	30	121	Matte	11	116
Mathis	3	2	Hill	9	29

7. When you compare the rushing performances of individual players, the average yards gained per carry is a better guide than the total of carries and yards gained. For the two players who gained most yards on each team, figure out the average yards gained per carry.
Strategy: This average is figured out the same way as the others —by dividing the number of yards gained by the number of carries.

When you have worked out these averages, you can list the four players in order from best to worst—this is called rank order, and it's an easy way to see the standings of the players in a game.
8. Using the final game statistics for passing (see page 24), you can now figure out the average yards gained per attempted pass for each of the three quarterbacks over the whole game. This is a good way to compare their play.
Strategy: Remember, the average yards per pass is found by dividing the total number of yards gained by the number of

PASSING, SUPER BOWL TOTALS

New York	passing attempts	yards gained	Baltimore	passing attempts	yards gained
Namath	28	206	Morrall	17	71
			Unitas	24	110

passes attempted. So for Namath, the problem would look like this: 206.00 ÷ 28 = ? Find the averages for Namath, Morrall, and Unitas.

9. To find the Colts' overall quarterbacking performance, you have to look at Morrall's and Unitas's combined statistics.

Strategy: Add Morrall's and Unitas's passing attempts and their yardage gained. Then divide to find their overall average yards per pass.

How did the Colts do overall compared with the Jets in average passing yardage?

RECEIVING, SUPER BOWL TOTALS

New York	catches	yards	Baltimore	catches	yards
Snell	4	40	Mackey	3	35
Lammons	2	13	Mitchell	1	15
Mathis	3	20	Richardson	6	58
Sauer	8	133	Matte	2	30
			Hill	2	1
			Orr	3	42

10. Another sportsmath statistic is for receivers—average yards per catch. For some of the receivers on each team, you may be able to figure out the averages in your head because the numbers divide evenly—try figuring out Snell's average, for instance. Mitchell's and Matte's averages are easy too. For the others you'll probably need a pencil and paper.

Strategy: To find a receiver's average yards per catch, divide the number of yards by the number of catches. Round off your answer to the nearest tenth.

11. Turner was in some ways the hero of the game for the Jets —he certainly scored the most points. Turner made five field goal attempts in the game; he missed two, one in the second quarter and one in the fourth, and he made three field goals for 32, 30, and 9 yards. What was his average yardage per field goal attempt?

Strategy: To find Turner's average yardage, divide the total yardage of the field goals by the number of field goal attempts.

Overtime

Here is a question that will show you how much sportsmath there really is in football.

When he had to decide whether to put Unitas into the game, Colt coach Don Shula might have wanted to compare Unitas's past performance with Morrall's and also with Namath's. Look at the chart on page 26 for these statistics.

Shula might have compared Unitas's and Morrall's lifetime average yardages per attempted pass; see if you can work out these averages.

Strategy: Work out these averages just like the others you have done, by dividing the total number of yards by the number of attempted passes.

25

PASSING

	lifetime attempted passes*	lifetime yardage gained*
Unitas	4129	33,160
Morrall	2046	15,717
Namath	1682	12,753

*Through the end of the 1968 season.

There isn't very much difference between Unitas's and Morrall's lifetime averages, although Unitas had thrown many more passes and gained much more total yardage since he had been playing a lot longer than Morrall. But Shula might also have looked at Morrall's performance in the Super Bowl's first half, and compared it with his lifetime average to see whether Morrall was having an off day. Compare the average you found in question 6 for Morrall's first half with the average you have just found for Morrall's lifetime; this is the kind of information coaches need to help them make decisions.

Football Sportsmath Answers

1.
$$9.17$$
$$317\overline{)2909.00}$$
Morrall averaged 9.2 yards per attempted pass in 1968.

$$8.28$$
$$380\overline{)3147.00}$$
Namath averaged 8.3 yards per attempted pass in 1968.

2.
$$3.95$$
$$91\overline{)360.00}$$
Hill averaged 4.0 yards per carry in 1968.

$$\begin{array}{r} 3.61 \\ 183\overline{)662.00} \end{array}$$ Matte averaged 3.6 yards per carry in 1968.

$$\begin{array}{r} 4.17 \\ 179\overline{)747.00} \end{array}$$ Snell averaged 4.2 yards per carry in 1968.

$$\begin{array}{r} 3.08 \\ 143\overline{)441.00} \end{array}$$ Boozer averaged 3.1 yards per carry in 1968.

3. $\quad\begin{array}{r} 15.57 \\ 28\overline{)436.00} \end{array}$ Michaels averaged 15.6 yards per field goal attempt in 1968.

$\quad\begin{array}{r} 19.50 \\ 46\overline{)897.00} \end{array}$ Turner averaged 19.5 yards per field goal attempt in 1968.

4. $\quad\begin{array}{r} 4.43 \\ 16\overline{)71.00} \end{array}$ Snell averaged 4.4 yards per carry in the first half of the Super Bowl.

$\quad\begin{array}{r} 15.20 \\ 5\overline{)76.00} \end{array}$ Matte averaged 15.2 yards per carry in the first half of the Super Bowl.

$\quad\begin{array}{r} 2.28 \\ 7\overline{)16.00} \end{array}$ Hill averaged 2.3 yards per carry in the first half of the Super Bowl.

5. $\quad\begin{array}{r} 6.93 \\ 16\overline{)111.00} \end{array}$ Namath averaged 6.9 yards per pass in the first half of the Super Bowl.

$\quad\begin{array}{r} 4.73 \\ 15\overline{)71.00} \end{array}$ Morrall averaged 4.7 yards per pass in the first half of the Super Bowl.

6. $\quad\begin{array}{r} 100 \\ -\ 20 \\ \hline 80 \text{ yards} \end{array}$ $\quad\begin{array}{r} 6.66 \\ 12\overline{)80.00} \end{array}$ Jets averaged 6.7 yards per play in this touchdown drive.

7. $\quad\begin{array}{r} 1.90 \\ 10\overline{)19.00} \end{array}$ Boozer averaged 1.9 yards per carry in the Super Bowl.

$\quad\begin{array}{r} 4.03 \\ 30\overline{)121.00} \end{array}$ Snell averaged 4.0 yards per carry in the Super Bowl.

$\quad\begin{array}{r} 10.54 \\ 11\overline{)116.00} \end{array}$ Matte averaged 10.5 yards per carry in the Super Bowl.

27

$$\begin{array}{r} 3.22 \\ 9\overline{)29.00} \end{array}$$

Hill averaged 3.2 yards per carry in the Super Bowl.

Rank order: Matte
Snell
Hill
Boozer

8.
$$\begin{array}{r} 7.35 \\ 28\overline{)206.00} \end{array}$$
Namath averaged 7.4 yards per pass in the Super Bowl.

$$\begin{array}{r} 4.17 \\ 17\overline{)71.00} \end{array}$$
Morrall averaged 4.2 yards per pass in the Super Bowl.

$$\begin{array}{r} 4.58 \\ 24\overline{)110.00} \end{array}$$
Unitas averaged 4.6 yards per pass in the Super Bowl.

9.
$$\begin{array}{r} 17 \\ +24 \\ \hline 41 \end{array} \qquad \begin{array}{r} 71 \\ +110 \\ \hline 181 \end{array} \qquad \begin{array}{r} 4.41 \\ 41\overline{)181.00} \end{array}$$

Morrall and Unitas together averaged 4.4 yards per pass, compared with Namath's 7.4 yards per pass.

10. Jets

$$\begin{array}{r} 10.00 \\ 4\overline{)40.00} \end{array}$$
Snell averaged 10.0 yards per catch in the Super Bowl.

$$\begin{array}{r} 6.50 \\ 2\overline{)13.00} \end{array}$$
Lammons averaged 6.5 yards per catch in the Super Bowl.

$$\begin{array}{r} 6.66 \\ 3\overline{)20.00} \end{array}$$
Mathis averaged 6.7 yards per catch in the Super Bowl.

$$\begin{array}{r} 16.62 \\ 8\overline{)133.00} \end{array}$$
Sauer averaged 16.6 yards per catch in the Super Bowl.

Colts

$$\begin{array}{r} 11.66 \\ 3\overline{)35.00} \end{array}$$
Mackey averaged 11.7 yards per catch in the Super Bowl.

$$\begin{array}{r} 15.00 \\ 1\overline{)15.00} \end{array}$$
Mitchell averaged 15.0 yards per catch in the Super Bowl.

          9.66   Richardson averaged 9.7 yards per catch in
6⟌58.00   the Super Bowl.

          15.00   Matte averaged 15.0 yards per catch in the
2⟌30.00   Super Bowl.

          0.50   Hill averaged 0.5 (or ½) yards per catch in
2⟌1.00   the Super Bowl.

          14.00   Orr averaged 14.0 yards per catch in the
3⟌42.00   Super Bowl.

11.   32
    30
    9
    0

Turner averaged 14.2 yards per

+ 0   14.20   field goal attempt in the Super
71   5⟌71.00   Bowl.

Overtime

               8.03   Unitas's lifetime average was 8.0
4129⟌33,160.00   yards per attempted pass.

               7.68   Morrall's lifetime average was 7.7
2046⟌15,717.00   yards per attempted pass.

               7.58   Namath's lifetime average was 7.6
1682⟌12,753.00   yards per attempted pass.

Morrall's first-half average in the Super Bowl was 4.7 yards
per attempted pass.

BASEBALL SPORTSMATH

There are probably more statistics about baseball in the newspapers than about any other sport. For teams and for individual players you can keep track of the number of runs batted in, home runs, errors, stolen bases, and all kinds of other baseball action. For pitchers, you can count the number of earned runs, wild pitches, hit batters, innings pitched, and just about anything else that pitchers do.

Some of the most important baseball statistics, however, are batting averages and fielding averages, for whole teams and for individual players. Even though they are called averages, these statistics are really percentages. Per cent means "per 100," so 90 per cent is the same as 90/100 or .90, and 100% is the same as 100/100 or 1.00. To make things more confusing, batting and fielding averages are worked out to three decimal places. If a player gets a hit every time he is at bat, his batting average is 100 per cent, but it is written as 1.000—in baseball this is called "batting a thousand."

Percentages are found by dividing the number of hits or outs made by the number of hits or outs attempted. The smaller number, therefore, is divided by the larger number—if the two numbers are the same, the answer is always 1.000 or 100 per cent.

Percentages are different from the.kinds of averages used in football sportsmath because they are found by using two numbers that refer to the same thing—for example, attempts to get a hit (these are called at-bats) and hits actually made. The numbers you use to find football averages refer to different things—for example, yards gained and passes attempted. But of course you could work out percentages for football too; you might

BASEBALL DIAMOND

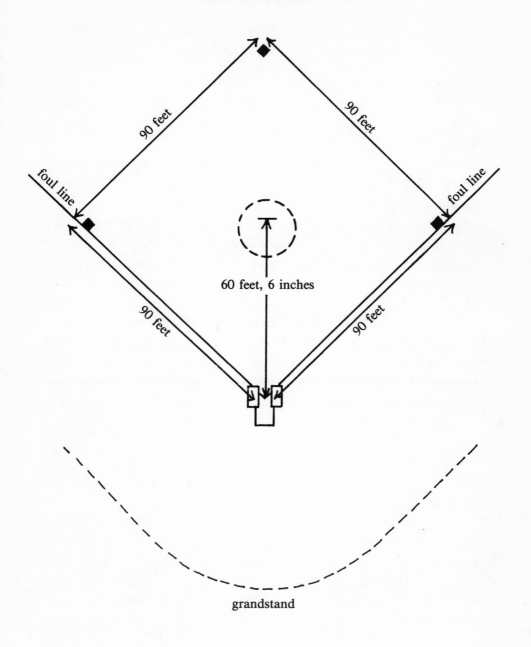

divide the number of completed passes by the number of attempted passes.

You can use the baseball facts given here to work out the sportsmath percentages for the 1974 World Series.

Baseball Facts

Time: 9 innings; no time limit

Field: diamond, 90 feet square; home plate to center field fence, about 400 feet

Scoring: 1 point for each run

Play: Each team comes up to bat in each inning. A team stays at bat until 3 outs have been made.

Number of players: 9 on each team on the field at any one time

Rosters for 1974 World Series

Oakland
Infield

Sal Bando
Bert Campaneris
Dick Green
Dal Maxvill
Gene Tenace
Manny Trillo

Outfield

Jesus Alou
Jim Holt
Reggie Jackson
Angel Mangual
Bill North
Joe Rudi
Claudell Washington

Los Angeles
Infield

Rick Auerbach
Ron Cey
Steve Garvey
Lee Lacy
Davey Lopes
Ken McMullen
Bill Russell

Outfield

Bill Buckner
Willie Crawford
Joe Ferguson
Von Joshua
Manny Mota
Tom Paciorek
Jim Wynn

Catcher	*Catcher*
Ray Fosse	Steve Yeager
Larry Haney	

Pitcher	*Pitcher*
Glenn Abbott	Jim Brewer
Vida Blue	Al Downing
Rollie Fingers	Charlie Hough
Ken Holtzman	Tommy John
Catfish Hunter	Mike Marshall
Darold Knowles	Andy Messersmith
Paul Lindblad	Doug Rau
Bob Locker	Eddie Solomon
Jim Odom	Don Sutton

Pinch runner

Herb Washington

World Series, 1974

The 1974 World Series was a clash between two West Coast teams as the Los Angeles Dodgers faced the two-time world champion Oakland A's.

It was the first time the Dodgers had made it to the Series in eight years, but they were slight favorites to win the championship. Their team statistics for the year were the best in the National League, with a team batting average of .272. The Dodgers were young, and eager to challenge the defending champs.

The Oakland A's, on the other hand, were hoping to join the New York Yankees in baseball record books as the only winners of three straight World Series titles. From their green and yellow uniforms and their bushy mustaches to their well-publicized squabbles among themselves, the Oakland players had the reputation of being a colorful and explosive team. Their pitching record for the year was the best in the American League, but their team batting average was well below the Dodgers', at .247. First in the American League in stolen bases, second in home runs, and third in runs scored, the A's had a total of 689 runs for the year—but the Dodgers had made 798 runs. It looked like a close contest.

The series opened in Los Angeles. Andy Messersmith, with a season record of 20 wins and 6 losses, pitched the opening game for the Dodgers. Ken Holtzman was on the mound for the A's.

The A's didn't take long to score, as Reggie Jackson clobbered a home run over the left field fence in the second inning. The score remained 1–0 for the A's until the fifth inning, when Oakland's starting pitcher Ken Holtzman cracked a double to left. He advanced to third on a wild pitch by Messersmith, and then scored on a bunt by Bert Campaneris. The A's were ahead by a margin of 2–0.

But Los Angeles came right back in the bottom of the fifth when Davey Lopes scored a run on two Oakland errors. No more runs came in until the top of the eighth when Campaneris, who had singled, scored on a wild throw by Dodger third base-man Ron Cey. The A's went ahead 3–1.

In the bottom of the ninth, with two outs, the Dodgers' Jim Wynn hit a home run to make it 3–2. Two Oakland players collided trying to chase the ball down. The Dodgers got the tying run on base but Catfish Hunter came in to get the final out— Oakland had won it 3–2.

The statistics for the first game of the series are shown in the chart on the next page.

1. See if you can figure out the batting averages for both teams to see which one did better at bat in this game.

Strategy: Remember that a batting average is really a percentage —you want to find out what percentage of the team's at-bats resulted in hits. To find Oakland's batting average, divide their

34

GAME 1

	at-bats	hits	put-outs	assists	errors
Oakland	28	6	27	10	2
Los Angeles	37	11	27	12	1

total hits (6) by their total at-bats (28). Work your answer to four decimal places and round it to the nearest thousandth. Then do the same for Los Angeles.

2. Now try to figure out the fielding average for each team in Game 1.

Strategy: A fielding average is also a percentage. It is the percentage of fielding plays, or chances for an out, that were successful. The total of fielding plays is found by adding the put-outs, assists, and errors. The number of *successful* fielding plays is found by adding the put-outs and assists only. (The errors are the fielding plays that were *not* successful.)

To find Oakland's fielding average, add their put-outs and assists: $27 + 10 = 37$. This is the number of successful fielding plays. Then add the errors to this sum to find the total number of fielding chances: $37 + 2 = 39$.

Divide the total fielding chances into the number of successful fielding plays: $37.0000 \div 39 = ?$ Again, work your answer to four decimal places and round to the nearest thousandth. Then work out the Dodgers' fielding average the same way.

It's interesting to see that Los Angeles did better in both batting and fielding, even though they lost this game. You might make charts like those on page 36 to show these averages. As you find the batting and fielding averages for the rest of the games in the series, you can enter them in the charts and compare them with one another.

BATTING AVERAGE

	Game 1	Game 2	Game 3	Game 4	Game 5	Series
Oakland						
Los Angeles						

FIELDING AVERAGE

	Game 1	Game 2	Game 3	Game 4	Game 5	Series
Oakland						
Los Angeles						

Game 2 matched tough Don Sutton, a 19-game winner for the Dodgers, against Vida Blue, Oakland's famous fastball thrower. As a record-breaking crowd of 55,989 looked on, the Dodgers' Ron Cey walked in the second inning and was advanced to second base by Bill Russell's single. Catcher Steve Yeager's single then allowed Cey to score, making it 1–0 for the Dodgers; Los Angeles held onto this lead for three more innings.

In the sixth inning Garvey singled for the Dodgers. Garvey had not been a regular at first base until the 1974 season. He was voted onto the All-Star team for that year by the fans in a write-in campaign, and was chosen Most Valuable Player in the All-Star game. He was also named Most Valuable Player in the National League for 1974. With Garvey on first, L.A.'s burly power hitter Joe Ferguson swatted a homer over the center field wall and the Dodgers were ahead 3–0. Oakland loaded the bases in the eighth, but Russell and Garvey pulled off a double play to end the inning.

Finally, in the ninth Oakland scored twice as Joe Rudi hit a single that brought in two runners. "Iron Mike" Marshall relieved Don Sutton on the pitcher's mound and quickly struck out Gene Tenace for Oakland's first out of the inning. The A's sent in Herb Washington as a pinch runner for Rudi at first base. But Iron Mike, known for his speed and his quick eye, picked off Washington with a throw to first and then struck out pinch hitter Angel Mangual for the final out in the game. The Dodgers had evened the series with a win of 3–2.

Here are the statistics for the second game:

GAME 2

	at-bats	hits	put-outs	assists	errors
Oakland	31	6	24	5	0
Los Angeles	29	6	27	9	1

3. You can figure out each team's batting average for this game and enter it on your chart.

Strategy: To find a batting average, divide the total number of hits by the total number of at-bats.

4. Now find the fielding average for each team in Game 2 and enter it on your chart.

Strategy: Add the put-outs and assists for each team to find the number of successful fielding plays. Then add the errors to this sum to find the total number of fielding chances. Divide the first number by the second to find the fielding average. (Can you figure out why Oakland had only 24 put-outs in a 9-inning game?)

The series was now tied at one game apiece. Both games had had low scores and the pitching had been tough. Baseball fans wondered when the power hitters on these teams would open up and start scoring. The A's were slightly favored to win the third game, which would be the first one played in Oakland. A sellout crowd of 49,347 was on hand at the Oakland Coliseum to see 27-game winner Jim "Catfish" Hunter go against the Dodgers' Al Downing.

Trouble for the Dodgers began in the third inning when Oakland's Reggie Jackson dribbled a ball up the first base line with two men on base. An error by Joe Ferguson (playing the catcher position for L.A. instead of his usual right field) allowed a run to score, and then a single by Joe Rudi made it 2–0.

In the fourth inning Dick Green, Oakland's second baseman, walked. On a sacrifice hit by Catfish Hunter, Green advanced to second base. Bert Campaneris followed with a crisp single to center; Green scored, and Oakland's lead was 3–0.

The Dodgers were scoreless until the eighth inning when Buckner homered for one run. Then in the ninth, Dodger right fielder Willie Crawford led off with a homer to right-center field. But a strike-out by relief pitcher Rollie Fingers and a double play ended the inning, and the A's had come away with another 3–2 victory.

GAME 3

	at-bats	hits	put-outs	assists	errors
Oakland	29	5	27	8	2
Los Angeles	33	7	24	10	2

5. The next column on your series charts can be filled in now with the batting and fielding averages from Game 3.

Strategy: For each team's batting average, divide the number of hits by the number of at-bats. For the fielding averages, divide

38

the total of put-outs and assists by the total of put-outs, assists, and errors.

Sportswriters and fans were beginning to call it a "ho-hum," boring series. Certainly the hitting had not been very exciting, and the fourth game was shaping up as another duel between two tough pitchers. It was a repeat of Game 1, as Andy Messersmith of the Dodgers went against Oakland's Ken Holtzman. Oakland was now ahead two games to one, and the managers of both teams had said that this fourth game would be crucial in winning the entire series.

The first two innings passed with no runs, but the Dodgers had a chance to score in the third inning when Steve Yeager hit a double off the left-center wall. Pitcher Andy Messersmith placed a bunt perfectly to advance Yeager to third. The next batter struck out, leaving Yeager still on third base. Then Bill Buckner tried a surprise bunt, but Holtzman threw Buckner out at first to put an end to the Dodger threat.

Holtzman doesn't bat during the regular season because of the American League's designated hitter rule, which allows a team to "designate" a tenth player whose only job is to bat for the pitcher. But in Oakland's half of the third inning Holtzman showed what he could do at the plate when he sent one of Messersmith's pitches sailing over the left field wall. The Oakland fans roared their approval as their team took the lead 1–0.

The Dodgers came right back in the fourth inning as Steve Garvey singled to right and Joe Ferguson walked. After Ron Cey struck out, Bill Russell came up and smacked a triple to right-center field. Now the Dodgers were ahead 2–1.

Nobody scored in the fifth inning, and it looked as if the hitting might be over for both teams. Neither team had scored more than three runs in the first three games of the series, and Messersmith had allowed only four hits so far in Game 4.

In the sixth, Messersmith walked Oakland's first batter, Bill

North. Messersmith didn't want North to advance into scoring position, so he tried several pickoff attempts to hold North close to first base. But his last pickoff throw was wild, and North dashed safely to second. Then Sal Bando, Oakland's third baseman and captain, drilled a single to right and North came home from second. It was Bando's first hit of the series, and the score was now 2–2.

Reggie Jackson was up next. The American League's Most Valuable Player of 1973, Jackson was one of baseball's most well-known and versatile stars. He was a power hitter who had hit 47 home runs in his second full season in the league. Though Jackson was injured with a pulled hamstring muscle, the Dodgers still considered him dangerous. He stood at the plate as Messersmith walked him on four pitches, putting runners on first and second with nobody out. Joe Rudi stepped up next and sacrifice bunted to put Bando on third and Jackson on second.

Many people were surprised to see Rudi bunt, since he had made only two sacrifices during the regular season. But it was sound strategy, moving the runners into scoring position in a close game.

Now Messersmith was really in trouble. He walked the next batter, Claudell Washington, intentionally to load the bases and set up a possible double play or a force-out at any base. This brought up Jim Holt, pinch-hitting for Oakland's catcher Ray Fosse. Holt's record as a pinch hitter was 0 for 26 times at bat, so the Dodgers expected a chance for at least one out. But with two strikes and the bases loaded, Holt smacked a solid hit to right field. Bando scored from third, and Reggie Jackson was racing around third for home plate as Joe Ferguson heaved a mighty throw from right field. Jackson slid around Dodger catcher Yeager, touching the plate as Yeager made the tag, and the umpire ruled, *"Safe!"* Yeager jumped up to argue about the call, but the television replay showed that Jackson's left foot had

40

Oakland's Reggie Jackson slides safely into the plate as Dodgers catcher Steve Yeager tries to make the tag in the sixth inning of the Series' Game 4. Sal Bando, at right, had already scored on Jim Holt's single. Yeager disputed the umpire's call on this costly play for the Dodgers.

United Press International Photo

touched the plate before Yeager tagged him. It was a close call, and an expensive play for the Dodgers. The A's now led 4–2 with only one out.

After the disputed play at home plate, Dick Green hit a bouncer to short. The Dodgers could only get one out on the play and Holt came in to score another run. It was 5–2 for the A's, the biggest lead either team had taken in the series so far. Finally Ken Holtzman rapped a ball straight to shortstop Bill Russell, and the long inning ended as Russell threw Holtzman out at first base.

41

The final out of Game 4 was a double play. Oakland's Dick Green (on the ground at left) scooped up Von Joshua's grounder and tossed it to Campaneris (number 19), forcing Ron Cey (on the ground at right) out at second. Campaneris relayed to first to get Joshua out and end the game.

United Press International Photo

After two scoreless innings, the Dodgers started a ninth inning rally when Ron Cey led off with a single. Rollie Fingers, who had relieved Holtzman on the mound, struck out the next Dodger batter, Bill Russell. Then Von Joshua came up, pinch-hitting for Steve Yeager. Oakland's second baseman Dick Green thought he knew where Joshua might hit the ball, and he chose his spot carefully. When Joshua smashed the ball, it looked like a sure base hit. But Green dove for the ball and tossed it underhand to

42

Bert Campaneris, who was covering second. Campaneris threw a bullet to first base and the game was over. The A's had capped their 5–2 win with a fantastic double play.

Now leading the series three games to one, the A's needed only one more game to capture their third World Series championship. It didn't take long, as Oakland scored quickly in Game 5 on a first inning error and a sacrifice fly. Ray Fosse increased the lead to 2–0 with a second inning home run.

The Dodgers put up a fight, tying the game at 2–2 in the sixth. But Oakland went ahead again in the seventh on Joe Rudi's home run into the left field bleachers. It turned out to be the last run of the year, as the A's hung onto their 3–2 margin to win the game and take their third World Series in a row.

The five-game series had been a close contest. You may be surprised to discover that the Dodgers' averages had often been better than Oakland's, and they had made only one more fielding error than the A's. But the Dodgers' errors had cost them runs, while the A's had managed to come through when it counted. In the important fourth game, the turning point for the series, Oakland's greater experience combined with some good luck had paved the way into the history books of baseball.

GAME 4				GAME 5		
	at-bats	hits			at-bats	hits
Oakland	26	7	Oakland	28	6
Los Angeles	32	7	Los Angeles	27	5

6. Using the statistics for Games 4 and 5, you can figure out both teams' batting averages and add them to your chart.

Strategy: For each team in each game, divide the number of hits by the number of at-bats to find the batting average.

SERIES BATTING

	Oakland at-bats	hits	Los Angeles at-bats	hits
Game 1	28	6	37	11
Game 2	31	6	29	6
Game 3	29	5	33	7
Game 4	26	7	32	7
Game 5	28	6	27	5

7. Now you can figure out the overall batting average in the series for each team. Enter these averages in your chart so you can compare the two teams' overall performance at the plate. **Strategy:** To find the batting averages for the series as a whole, add the number of at-bats and the number of hits for each team. Then divide the total of each team's hits by its total of at-bats.

INDIVIDUAL BATTING

Oakland	at-bats	hits	Los Angeles	at-bats	hits
Campaneris	17	6	Garvey	21	8
Rudi	18	6	Yeager	11	4
Holtzman	4	2	Messersmith	4	2

8. You may want to figure out some of the individual players' batting averages. From the figures given in the chart, you can find batting averages for the big hitters of the series on each team, and also for two of the pitchers.

Since pitchers don't play in every game and often don't stay in for a complete game, they don't have as many chances to make hits as the other players. But they are usually considered poor hitters, and Holtzman doesn't even bat during the season, so their averages may surprise you.

Strategy: You find a player's batting average in the same way you find a team's batting average—by dividing the number of hits by the number of at-bats.

Extra Innings

To compare how the two teams performed in the field, you can figure out each team's fielding average for the whole series.

Strategy: First add up the totals of put-outs, assists, and errors for all five games. Then add the total put-outs and assists only, and divide this sum by the total put-outs, assists, and errors.

SERIES FIELDING

	Oakland put-outs	assists	errors	Los Angeles put-outs	assists	errors
Game 1	27	10	2	27	12	1
Game 2	24	5	0	27	9	1
Game 3	27	8	2	24	10	2
Game 4	27	14	0	24	13	1
Game 5	27	14	1	24	6	1

Baseball Sportsmath Answers

1.

$$28\overline{)6.0000} \quad .2142$$

Oakland's batting average in Game 1 was .214.

$$37\overline{)11.0000} \quad .2972$$

Los Angeles's batting average in Game 1 was .297.

2.

$$39\overline{)37.0000} \quad .9487$$

Oakland's fielding average in Game 1 was .949.

$$\begin{array}{r} 27 \\ +12 \\ \hline 39 \end{array} \qquad \begin{array}{r} 39 \\ + 1 \\ \hline 40 \end{array} \qquad 40\overline{)39.0000} \quad .9750$$

Los Angeles's fielding average in Game 1 was .975.

3.

$$31\overline{)6.0000} \quad .1935$$

Oakland's batting average in Game 2 was .194.

$$29\overline{)6.0000} \quad .2068$$

Los Angeles's batting average in Game 2 was .207.

4.

$$\begin{array}{r} 24 \\ + 5 \\ \hline 29 \end{array} \qquad \begin{array}{r} 29 \\ + 0 \\ \hline 29 \end{array} \qquad 29\overline{)29.0000} \quad 1.0000$$

Oakland's fielding average in Game 2 was 1.000.

$$\begin{array}{r} 27 \\ + 9 \\ \hline 36 \end{array} \qquad \begin{array}{r} 36 \\ + 1 \\ \hline 37 \end{array} \qquad 37\overline{)36.0000} \quad .9729$$

Los Angeles's fielding average in Game 2 was .973.

5.

$$29\overline{)5.0000} \quad .1724$$

Oakland's batting average in Game 3 was .172.

$$33\overline{)7.0000} \quad .2121$$

Los Angeles's batting average in Game 3 was .212.

$$\begin{array}{r} 27 \\ + 8 \\ \hline 35 \end{array} \qquad \begin{array}{r} 35 \\ + 2 \\ \hline 37 \end{array} \qquad 37\overline{)35.0000} \quad .9459$$

Oakland's fielding average in Game 3 was .946.

```
  24        34
 +10       + 2              .9444
  34        36       36 ⌐34.0000
```

Los Angeles's fielding average in Game 3 was .944.

6.   .2692   Oakland's batting average in Game 4 was
       26 ⌐7.0000   .269.
            .2142   Oakland's batting average in Game 5 was
       28 ⌐6.0000   .214.
            .2187   Los Angeles's batting average in Game 4 was
       32 ⌐7.0000   .219.
            .1851   Los Angeles's batting average in Game 5 was
       27 ⌐5.0000   .185.

```
7.     28          6
       31          6
       29          5
       26          7
     + 28        + 6                  .2112
      142         30        142 ⌐30.0000
```

Oakland's batting average for the series was .211.

```
       37         11
       29          6
       33          7
       32          7
     + 27        + 5                  .2278
      158         36        158 ⌐36.0000
```

Los Angeles's batting average for the series was .228.

8.   .3529   Campaneris's batting average for the series
       17 ⌐6.0000   was .353.
            .3333   Rudi's batting average for the series was
       18 ⌐6.0000   .333.
            .5000   Holtzman's batting average for the series was
        4 ⌐2.0000   .500.

47

$$\begin{array}{r} .3809 \\ 21\overline{\smash{\big)}8.0000} \end{array}$$ Garvey's batting average for the series was .381.

$$\begin{array}{r} .3636 \\ 11\overline{\smash{\big)}4.0000} \end{array}$$ Yeager's batting average for the series was .364.

$$\begin{array}{r} .5000 \\ 4\overline{\smash{\big)}2.0000} \end{array}$$ Messersmith's batting average for the series was .500.

Extra Innings

27	10	2		
24	5	0		
27	8	2		
27	14	0	132	183
+ 27	+14	+1	+ 51	+ 5
132	51	5	183	188

$$\begin{array}{r} .9734 \\ 188\overline{\smash{\big)}183.0000} \end{array}$$ Oakland's fielding average for the series was .973.

27	12	1		
27	9	1		
24	10	2		
24	13	1	126	176
+ 24	+ 6	+1	+ 50	+ 6
126	50	6	176	182

$$\begin{array}{r} .9670 \\ 182\overline{\smash{\big)}176.0000} \end{array}$$ Los Angeles's fielding average for the series was .967.

BASKETBALL SPORTSMATH

In the fast-moving game of professional basketball, the score of a game can add up to a much higher number than a score in football or baseball. But in the record books of basketball, final scores are often less important than averages and percentages. The average number of points a player makes per game tells you how good his shooting is over a whole season. And his shooting percentage gives you information on how hot he is in a particular game.

Of course, when a player makes high scores, his averages and percentages go up too. You can use basketball sportsmath to figure out some averages and percentages for the all-time high scorer in basketball, Wilt Chamberlain.

Basketball Facts (NBA rules)

Time: 4 quarters, 12 minutes playing time each
Court: 94 feet long, 50 feet wide
Scoring: 2 points for every basket (field goal);
      1 point for every free throw (foul shot)
Number of players: 5 players on the court for each team at one
      time

Rosters for March 2, 1962

Philadelphia Warriors

Arizin (starting forward)
Meschery (starting forward)

New York Knicks

Green (starting forward)
Naulls (starting forward)

Chamberlain (center)	Imhoff (center)
Attles (starting guard)	Butler (starting guard)
Rodgers (starting guard)	Guerin (starting guard)
Conlin	Buckner
Larese	Budd
Luckenbill	Butcher
Ruklik	

Chamberlain's Big Game

Wilt Chamberlain was the greatest scorer in the history of professional basketball. Wilt's size (7'1", 275 pounds) and skill made him a valuable asset to every team he played on. It sometimes seemed that the Big Dipper, as he was called, could score any time he wanted.

After two years at Kansas State University, Wilt played with the Harlem Globetrotters for a year before signing with the NBA's Philadelphia Warriors for the 1959–60 season. In his rookie year he led the league in scoring: he played 72 games and scored 2707 points for an average of 37.6 points per game. No player had ever before averaged more than 30 points a game. In this same season Cincinnati's Jack Twyman also passed the 30-point mark, averaging 31.2 points a game, but Wilt's fantastic average crowded Twyman out of the top spot.

In his second year Wilt went on to break his own records of the previous season: he played in 79 games and scored 3033 points for an average of 38.4 points per game. The basketball world had never seen anything like it. Fans began to wonder what Wilt could do as he gained more experience in the pro league. And they found out on March 2, 1962, near the end of Wilt's third season in the NBA.

NBA games were sometimes played on neutral courts so that more people could see the stars like Wilt play. In these games neither team was home team. The game on March 2, 1962, was played in Hershey, Pennsylvania, between the Philadelphia

BASKETBALL COURT

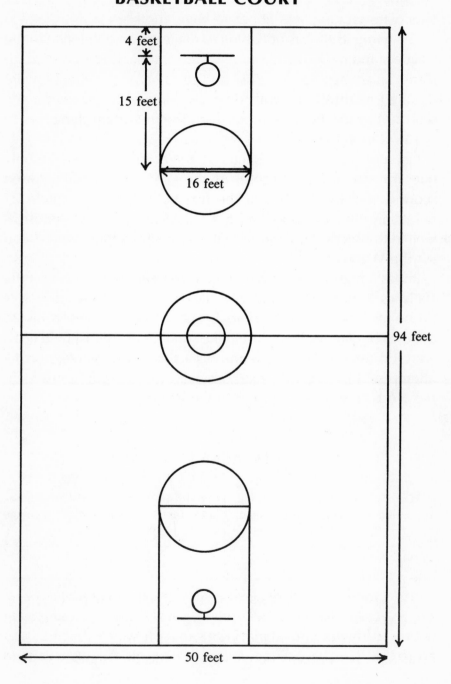

4 feet

15 feet

16 feet

94 feet

50 feet

Warriors and the New York Knicks. Hershey, known best for its chocolate factory, was about to have another claim to fame.

The game itself was not going to make much difference to the league standings. The Warriors were on their way to a second-place finish behind the Boston Celtics, and the Knicks were doomed to finish last with only 29 wins in 80 games for the season. But for the fans in Hershey, the important thing was to see Wilt in action.

Just about everyone expected the Warriors to win—the only question was the final score. As the game began, Wilt started scoring, and by the end of the first quarter he had made 23 points and the Warriors had a 42–26 lead. Wilt did almost as well in the second quarter, and the score at halftime was 79–68 for the Warriors.

It was a high score for halftime; as the announcer read off the statistics, it turned out that Wilt had made 41 of Philadelphia's 79 points. He had 14 field goals and 13 free throws in his 24 minutes of play. Wilt was pretty hot that night. His 14 field goals were on only 26 attempts, and his 13 free throws were on 14 attempts. This was really extraordinary, for Wilt was considered the worst free-throw shooter in the league.

CHAMBERLAIN'S FIRST HALF

field goals attempted	field goals made	field goal shooting percentage	free throws attempted	free throws made	free throw percentage
26	14		14	13	

1. The chart shows Wilt's statistics for the first half of the game. See if you can figure out his shooting percentage (percentage of field goals or baskets made) for the first half.
Strategy: To find this percentage, divide the number of field

goals (or baskets) made by the number of field goals attempted. Work the answer to three decimal places and round to the nearest hundredth. The problem for Wilt's first half shooting percentage would look like this: 14.000 ÷ 26 = ?

2. You can also work out Wilt's free throw percentage for the first half.

Strategy: To find Wilt's free throw percentage for the first half, divide the number of free throws made by the number of free throws attempted. Again, work the answer to three decimal places and round to the nearest hundredth.

With 41 points at the half, Wilt had a chance to break the record for the most points scored in a single professional basketball game. The record belonged to Elgin Baylor of the Minneapolis Lakers, who had made 71 points in one game in 1960. If Wilt kept up his scoring pace in the second half, he could break Baylor's record. Wilt wasn't likely to come out of the game—he rarely missed even a minute of play and had never fouled out of a game. Unless his shooting cooled off, his chances for a record score looked good.

Wilt stayed hot in the third quarter, which ended with the Warriors in front 125–106. Wilt had taken 16 shots and made 10 of them, and had been 8 for 8 from the foul line—28 points in all for the third quarter and 69 for the game so far.

As the fourth quarter got under way, the fans were concentrating on every move. Only two points were between Wilt and Baylor's record, and he scored them almost at once. The record-breaking field goal followed almost immediately, and Wilt's score stood at 73 points.

The Warriors were pulling away with a lead of nearly 20 points. The only remaining question was—how many points would Wilt rack up? All Philadelphia's passes were to Wilt as the Warriors concentrated on his shooting. The Knicks put three men on him but he was too strong.

Wilt Chamberlain (number 13) goes in for a layup in a game against the Knicks on March 4, 1962—two days after his 100-point game at Hershey. At left is Naulls (number 6) of the Knicks, and at right is Arizin (number 11) of the Warriors. Wilt "only" made 58 points in this game, which the Warriors won 129-128.

United Press International Photo

Usually the opposing team could keep Wilt from scoring too much by fouling him. He was so poor from the foul line—generally making only about 50 per cent of his free throws—that fouling him was certain to cost fewer points than letting him take shots. But in this game fouling Wilt didn't help the Knicks. He had never been so accurate from the foul line.

Wilt kept on shooting and scoring through the fourth quarter. Finally, with less than a minute to go in the game, the score was 167–147. And Wilt had 98 points! He had made 7 out of 10 free throws in the fourth quarter, and he had made 11 out of 20 attempts at field goals.

With 42 seconds remaining, Wilt took another shot—and made it! *One hundred points!* The fans roared as the game ended at 169–147. It had been the greatest scoring exhibition in the history of basketball.

CHAMBERLAIN'S GAME TOTALS

	field goals attempted (FGA)	field goals made (FGM)	field goal percentage (FG%)	free throws attempted (FTA)	free throws made (FTM)	free throw percentage (FT%)
1st quarter	14	7		9	9	
2nd quarter	12	7		5	4	
1st half	26	14	54	14	13	93
3rd quarter	16	10		8	8	
4th quarter	21	12		10	7	
2nd half	37	22		18	15	
total	63	36		32	28	

3. Using the chart on page 55, you can figure out Wilt's field goal percentage for the whole game. Also figure out his percentage for the second half or for each quarter if you want to compare them. You can make a chart of your own and fill in the numbers as you work them out.

Strategy: To find the field goal percentage, divide the number of field goals made by the number of field goals attempted.

4. You can also figure out Wilt's free throw percentage for the whole game (or for the quarters and halves) and compare it with his lifetime percentage of approximately 50 percent.

Strategy: To find this percentage, divide the number of free throws Wilt made by the number of free throws he attempted.

5. Using the team scoring charts below, you can figure out the shooting percentage for each team as a whole.

TEAM SCORING

Philadelphia	FGA	FGM	FG%	FTA	FTM	FT%
Arizin	18	7		2	2	
Meschery	12	7		2	2	
Chamberlain	63	36		32	28	
Attles	8	8		1	1	
Rodgers	4	1		12	9	
Conlin	4	0		0	0	
Larese	5	4		1	1	
Luckenbill	0	0		0	0	
Ruklik	1	0		2	0	
total						

New York	FGA	FGM	FG%	FTA	FTM	FT%
Green	7	3		0	0	
Naulls	22	9		15	13	
Imhoff	7	3		1	1	
Butler	13	4		0	0	
Guerin	29	13		17	13	
Buckner	26	16		1	1	
Budd	8	6		1	1	
Butcher	6	3		6	4	
total						

Strategy: First you have to add up each column to find the totals of field goals attempted and field goals made. Then divide the number of field goals made by the whole team by the number of field goals attempted.

6. You can also figure out the free throw percentage for each team.

Strategy: Again, add up each column to find the totals of free throws attempted and free throws made. Then divide the number of free throws made by the whole team by the number of free throws attempted.

7. In 1961–62, the season of his 100-point game, Wilt broke every scoring record in pro basketball. He made 4029 points in 80 games.

With these facts you can figure out Wilt's average score per game for the 1961–62 season.

Strategy: To find the average, divide the number of points scored by the number of games played. Work the problem to two decimal places and then round to the nearest tenth. The problem for Wilt's 1961–62 season would look like this: $4029.00 \div 80 = ?$

CHAMBERLAIN'S AVERAGE SCORES

	number of games	number of points	average
1959–60	72	2707	37.6
1960–61	79	3033	38.4
1961–62	80	4029	
total			

8. Now you can figure out Wilt's average score per game for his first three seasons in the NBA.

Strategy: Add up each of the first two columns to find the total number of games and the total number of points for the three seasons. Then divide the number of points by the number of games to find the overall average to the nearest tenth.

You might think that you could find this average more easily by adding the average scores for the three seasons and dividing this total by three. But if you try doing it this way, you will see that the answer you get is not really accurate.

9. The rest of the Warriors didn't have very impressive scores in this game—they were too busy passing to Wilt. You can figure out the average score for the rest of Wilt's team from the chart on the next page.

Strategy: To find an average of this kind, first add all the Warriors' scores except Wilt's. Then divide this total by the number of players (assume that each member of the team played in this game).

Another way of doing this, since you know what Wilt's score was and you know Philadelphia's final score, is to subtract Wilt's score from the team's total. Then all you need to know is how many other players were on the team, and you're ready to divide.

INDIVIDUAL SCORES

Warriors	points	Knicks	points
Arizin	16	Green	6
Meschery	16	Naulls	31
Attles	17	Imhoff	7
Rodgers	11	Butler	8
Conlin	0	Guerin	39
Larese	9	Buckner	33
Luckenbill	0	Budd	13
Ruklik	0	Butcher	10

10. You've probably realized that the Knicks had to have a higher scoring average than the Warriors (without Wilt), since they didn't have a 100-point player. They were able to make a high final score partly because the Warriors were concentrating on Wilt's scoring rather than on defense. You can figure out the Knicks' average score and compare it with the Warriors' average score (not including Wilt).

Strategy: Again, divide the Knicks' total score by the number of players on the team to find the team's average score for the game.

Overtime

Wilt has been one of the NBA's highest-paid players. In 1967–68 he was reported to have a salary of $250,000.00 for the regular season. Just for fun, figure out Wilt's salary per game if he played 80 games in that season.

Strategy: This is another averaging problem. To find Wilt's pay per game, divide his total salary by the number of games he played.

If Wilt played every minute of every game in that season, how much did he make per minute?

Strategy: Since there are 48 minutes in a game, you can multiply the number of minutes per game by the number of games to find the total number of minutes. Then divide Wilt's salary by this total.

Another way to find the answer, since you already know how much Wilt made per game, is to divide that number by 48—this will tell you how much he made in one minute of one game.

It sure sounds like a lot of money—but of course this doesn't include practice and travel time, just playing time.

Basketball Sportsmath Answers

1. $\dfrac{.538}{26 \overline{)14.000}}$ 54% field goal shooting for Wilt in first half

2. $\dfrac{.928}{14 \overline{)13.000}}$ 93% free throw shooting for Wilt in first half

3. $\dfrac{.500}{14 \overline{)7.000}}$ 50% field goal shooting for Wilt in first quarter

    $\dfrac{.583}{12 \overline{)7.000}}$ 58% field goal shooting for Wilt in second quarter

    $\dfrac{.625}{16 \overline{)10.000}}$ 63% field goal shooting for Wilt in third quarter

    $\dfrac{.571}{21 \overline{)12.000}}$ 57% field goal shooting for Wilt in fourth quarter

    $\dfrac{.594}{37 \overline{)22.000}}$ 59% field goal shooting for Wilt in second half

                .571   57% field goal shooting for Wilt in entire
        63 ⟌36.000   game

4.   1.000   100% free throw shooting for Wilt in first
        9 ⟌9.000   quarter
                .800   80% free throw shooting for Wilt in second
        5 ⟌4.000   quarter
              1.000   100% free throw shooting for Wilt in third
        8 ⟌8.000   quarter
                .700   70% free throw shooting for Wilt in fourth
      10 ⟌7.000   quarter
                .833   83% free throw shooting for Wilt in second
      18 ⟌15.000   half
                .875   88% free throw shooting for Wilt in entire
      32 ⟌28.000   game

5. **Philadelphia**   **New York**

field goals attempted	field goals made	field goals attempted	field goals made
18	7	7	3
12	7	22	9
63	36	7	3
8	8	13	4
4	1	29	13
4	0	26	16
5	4	8	6
0	0	+ 6	+ 3
+ 1	+ 0	118	57
115	63		

            .547   .483
115 ⟌63.000   118 ⟌57.000

55% field goal shooting   48% field goal shooting
for Philadelphia   for New York

61

6. Philadelphia   New York

free throws attempted	free throws made	free throws attempted	free throws made
2	2	0	0
2	2	15	13
32	28	1	1
1	1	0	0
12	9	17	13
0	0	1	1
1	1	1	1
0	0	+ 6	+ 4
+ 2	+ 0	41	33
52	43		

$$52\overline{)43.000}\;\;.826 \qquad 41\overline{)33.000}\;\;.804$$

83% free throw shooting
for Philadelphia

80% free throw shooting
for New York

7. $80\overline{)4029.00}\;\;50.36$ 50.4 average points per game for Wilt in
1961–62 season

8.

72	2707
79	3033
+ 80	+4029
231	9769

$$231\overline{)9769.00}\;\;42.29$$

42.3 average points per game for Wilt's first three seasons
in the NBA

OR

37.6
38.4
+ 50.4
126.4

$$3\overline{)126.40}\;\;42.13$$ 42.1 average points
per game

9.

```
        16
        16
        17
        11
         0
         9
         0              169
     +   0             -100              8.62
        69      OR      69          8 ⟌69.00
```

8.6 average points for Warriors, not including Wilt

10.

```
         6
        31
         7
         8
        39
        33
        13
     +  10            18.37      18.4 average points for Knicks
       147        8 ⟌147.00
```

Overtime

```
            $3,125.00           $3,125.00 per game
     80 ⟌$250,000.00
```

```
         48
      ×  80                     $65.10      OR              $65.10
       3840       3840 ⟌$250,000.00              48 ⟌$3125.00
     $65.10 per minute of play
```

HOCKEY SPORTSMATH

Hockey, like other professional sports, uses a lot of numbers. For example, you can figure out the percentage of shots made by a team or an individual player, or the percentage of saves made by a goalie.

A lot of hockey sportsmath involves just adding and subtracting, but it's a little complicated because you're often adding and subtracting minutes and seconds. Penalties are an important part of every hockey game and you may frequently want to figure out how much time is left in a penalty or in two different penalties.

After you do the sportsmath for the game between New York and Detroit at the end of the 1970 season, you'll be able to keep track of any hockey games you watch, along with the statisticians.

Hockey Facts

Time: 3 periods, 20 minutes playing time each
Rink: 200 feet long, 85 feet wide
Scoring: Each goal counts 1 point.
Number of players: 6 players on the ice at any one time for each team (except during a penalty)

Rosters for April 5, 1970

Detroit	New York
Forwards	*Forwards*
Wayne Connelly	Dave Balon

64

Gary Croteau	Jack Egers
Billy Dea	Bill Fairbairn
Alex Delvecchio	Rod Gilbert
Gordie Howe	Ted Irvine
Al Karlander	Orland Kurtenbach
Nick Libett	Don Luce
Bruce MacGregor	Bob Nevin
Frank Mahovlich	Jean Ratelle
Pete Stemkowski	Ron Stewart
Garry Unger	Walt Tkaczuk

Defensemen	*Defensemen*
Bobby Baun	Arnie Brown
Gary Bergman	Larry Brown
Carl Brewer	Ab DeMarco
Ron Harris	Allan Hamilton
Paul Popiel	Tim Horton
Dale Rolfe	Jim Neilson
	Brad Park
	Rod Seiling

Goalkeepers	*Goalkeepers*
Roger Crozier	Ed Giacomin
Roy Edwards	Terry Sawchuk

Injured	*Injured*
None	Vic Hadfield
	Don Marshall

The Rangers' Last Chance

"Never give up."

"The impossible can happen."

"The game's not over until the final buzzer."

All these old sayings came true on a Sunday afternoon in New York City when the New York Rangers faced the Detroit Red Wings in one of the most exciting hockey games ever played.

It was April 5, 1970, the final day of the NHL's seven-month

ICE HOCKEY RINK

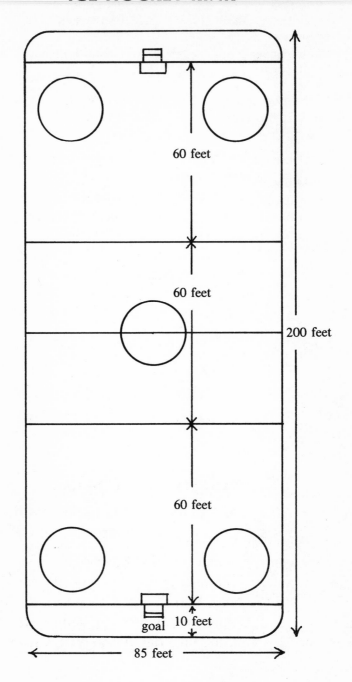

season. After this Sunday's games, the top four teams in the standings would go on to the playoffs, hoping to win the Stanley Cup and become the season's champions.

A difficult schedule and hectic pace had taken their toll on the Rangers and they were weary. Today's game was their last chance to make the playoffs, and it wasn't going to be easy. The night before—Saturday, April 4—they had been beaten in Detroit by a 6–2 score. And they would be playing their last game in the afternoon, after flying home from Detroit and getting to sleep around 4:30 in the morning.

The Rangers' only hope was to defeat Detroit on Sunday, while at the same time Chicago defeated Montreal, the team currently in fourth place. This would create a tie between Montreal and New York for the fourth position in the standings. And that wasn't all—if they did finish in a tie, the playoff spot would be awarded to the fourth-place team that had the most goals for the season. So the Rangers not only had to win while the Canadiens lost; they had to score more goals than Montreal in order to pass them in total goals scored for the season.

1. Before the game started on April 5, New York had 237 total goals for the season. Montreal had 242. How many goals did the Rangers have to score that day to pass Montreal in total goals scored?
Strategy: Subtract the Rangers' total goals from Montreal's total goals. This will tell you how many goals the Rangers needed to tie Montreal. Then add 1 to this number to find out how many goals the Rangers needed to pass Montreal in total goals.

Of course, the number of goals you found the Rangers needed is the number they would need if Montreal didn't score at all against Chicago that day. If Montreal did score, the Rangers would have to make the same number of goals Montreal did, *plus* the number they needed to pass Montreal's total.

67

This was a tall order for the weary and just-beaten Rangers, and they had no way of knowing whether the Canadiens would be really hot against Chicago. To make matters worse, some of New York's players were out with injuries. Still, Ranger coach Emile Francis had his team in good spirits as they warmed up for the Sunday match. Hockey fans all over the country were watching, since the game was on national television. And, though many Ranger fans believed that the situation was hopeless, every seat in Madison Square Garden was filled.

The Rangers began the game skating hard, attacking Detroit goalie Roger Crozier. They got a shot off after just 18 seconds and barely missed—18 seconds later right wing Rod Gilbert shot and scored to put the Rangers ahead 1–0.

Gilbert, the Rangers' all-time leading scorer, was also known as a clever playmaker. His boyhood friend Jean Ratelle played on the same line as Gilbert and was credited with an assist on Gilbert's goal.

Detroit's Gary Bergman made the next goal to tie the game. But at 8:25 in the first period Jack Egers scored a goal for the Rangers, and at 12:21 Dave Balon also scored. It was the first time in nearly two months that the Rangers had scored three goals in one period.

The fans began to think that a miracle was possible after all. But the Montreal-Chicago game would not be played until that evening, so all the Rangers could do was to try to pile up points. This was not an easy task, especially since they didn't have a firm total to shoot for; the Canadiens might not score at all against Chicago, or they might win by a huge margin. The Rangers just kept on skating hard and taking shots.

At 17:48 in the first period Egers scored again. Egers had been brought up from the minor league team in Omaha to play in this game because of the Rangers' injuries, and he was certainly playing a good game. When the first period ended, the Rangers were on top 4–1.

Action around the Detroit goal, as Rod Gilbert (number 7) of the Rangers has the puck behind the net. Teammate Jack Egers (number 20) is at right.

United Press International Photo

2. How much time was left in the first period after Egers's goal at 17:48?

Strategy: You know there are 20 minutes in a period and 60 seconds in a minute. To find out how much time was left, subtract the time of Egers's goal from the total minutes in the period. Since you aren't working only with whole minutes, you can write 20 minutes as 19:60 (19 minutes and 60 seconds) to make subtracting easier.

3. The chart on page 70 shows the important action of the first period of the game. In hockey, each goal and each assist counts 1 point in figuring out the players' point totals for the season. Which New York player made the most points in the first period?

Strategy: Since each goal and each assist counts as 1 point, add up the number of goals and assists for each Ranger listed.

Scoring   *Penalties*

Team	Goal	Assist	Assist	Time	Team	Penalty	Infraction	Time
N.Y.	Gilbert	Ratelle	A. Brown	0:36	Det.	Stemkowski	Hooking	6:26
Det.	Bergman	Connelly	Libett	3:08	Det.	Karlander	Holding	12:07
N.Y.	Egers	Nevin	A. Brown	8:25				
N.Y.	Balon	Tkaczuk	A. Brown	12:31				
N.Y.	Egers	Horton		17:48				

4. The chart also shows you when penalties were called on Detroit in the first period (New York had no penalties in this period). When a penalty is called against a player, he must go to the penalty box at the sideline for a certain length of time. During this time his team plays "short-handed," with only five men including the goalie on the ice.

Hooking and holding are usually minor penalties that last 2 minutes; major penalties are 5 minutes long.

Assuming that both of Detroit's penalties were 2-minute penalties, you can figure out whether the Rangers scored any goals when Detroit was playing short-handed. If any goals were scored during the penalties, how much time was left in the penalty when the goal was scored?

Strategy: First add 2 minutes to the time of the first penalty against Detroit to find out when the penalty would be over. For the first penalty in the first period, the problem would look like this: 6:26

      $\underline{+2:00}$

      8:26.

Now check to see whether the Rangers scored any goals between the time the penalty was called and the time it would be over. If they did, subtract the time of the New York goal from the time when the penalty would end:

$$
\begin{array}{r}
8{:}26 \\
-\,8{:}25 \\
\hline
0{:}01.
\end{array}
$$

This means that one second of Stemkowski's penalty was left to be served when Egers scored. It was the Rangers' last chance for a power play!

Now do the same for Detroit's second penalty in the period to see whether New York scored again when Detroit was short-handed and how much time was left in the penalty. This will give you an idea of how important penalties can be in a hockey game.

In the second period the Rangers kept up the pressure. After only 20 seconds Gilbert scored again—New York's fifth goal. This meant that if the Canadiens were shut out later in Chicago, the Rangers would finish the season in fourth place. But they couldn't count on a shutout.

Shot after shot they fired, and the Rangers' Ron Stewart scored goals at 7:38 and 18:35 in the second period. Mahovlich and Stemkowski also scored for Detroit to make it 7–3 at the end of the second period.

In the third and final period, Balon added two goals at 1:21 and 9:48, giving him three for the day (a "hat trick" in hockey). Howe and Libett scored for Detroit, making the final score 9–5 in favor of New York. It was an amazingly high-scoring game; the fans and even the Rangers themselves couldn't believe what their team had accomplished.

That night every Ranger fan's radio was tuned to the Montreal-Chicago game. Even with the Rangers' fantastic score of 9 goals, Montreal could still beat them in total goals for the season and go on to the playoffs.

But as the Montreal-Chicago game went on, Ranger fans stopped worrying. Chicago, the first-place team, had little diffi-

The Rangers' Dave Balon (number 17) in action against the Red Wings in the big game on April 5, 1970.

United Press International Photo

culty in defeating the Canadiens. In fact, they outdid the Rangers and downed Montreal 10–2, putting the Canadiens in fifth place and out of the playoffs. New York had done the impossible— they would now go on to the Stanley Cup competition!

5. To pass the Rangers in total goals, how many goals would Montreal have had to score on Sunday night?

Strategy: Remember that before Sunday's games New York had 237 goals for the season and Montreal had 242. First find the

Rangers' new season total by adding the goals they scored against Detroit to their previous total.

Then subtract Montreal's total goals before Sunday's game from the Rangers' new total. This tells you how many goals Montreal would have needed to tie the Rangers. Add 1 to your answer to find the number of goals Montreal would have needed to make the playoffs.

There is another way to do this problem. Since you already know from problem 1 on page 67 how many goals the Rangers needed to tie Montreal, you can subtract this number from the number of goals the Rangers actually made. This will tell you how many goals Montreal would have needed to tie the Rangers' new total.

6. The game chart on the next page is like those that are used at NHL games. It shows the important events in this hockey game. You might want to make a chart like this to fill in the next time you watch a hockey game.

Using the game chart, you can figure out how many points each player made in this game. Who were the three high scorers?

Strategy: Since you know that each goal and each assist counts 1 point in the players' point totals, add up the number of goals and assists for each player who made points in the game.

7. You can also figure out from the game chart whether any goals in the second and third periods were scored when the opposing team was short-handed, assuming that all the penalties were 2-minute penalties.

Strategy: You can probably work this out in your head. Add 2 minutes to the time of each penalty, and then look at the chart to see whether the opposing team scored any goals between the time the penalty was called and the time it would be over.

8. While you were figuring out the last sportsmath problem, you may have noticed that in the third period each team scored one

GAME CHART

April 5, 1970: New York Rangers vs. Detroit Red Wings

		Scoring						Penalties		
	Team	Goal	Assist	Assist	Time	Team	Penalty	Infraction	Time
1st per.	N.Y.	Gilbert	Ratelle	A. Brown	0:36	Det.	Stemkowski	Hooking	6:26
	Det.	Bergman	Connelly	Libett	3:08	Det.	Karlander	Holding	12:07
	N.Y.	Egers	Nevin	A. Brown	8:25				
	N.Y.	Balon	Tkaczuk	A. Brown	12:31				
	N.Y.	Egers	Horton		17:48				
2nd per.	N.Y.	Gilbert	Ratelle	Park	0:20	Det.	Harris	Charging	0:36
	Det.	Mahovlich	Delvecchio	Brewer	4:21	Det.	Unger	Hooking	12:05
	N.Y.	Stewart	Kurtenbach	Nevin	7:38				
	N.Y.	Stewart	A. Brown	Kurtenbach	18:35				
	Det.	Stemkowski	MacGregor		19:01				
3rd per.	N.Y.	Balon	unassisted		1:21	N.Y.	Seiling	Holding	1:31
	N.Y.	Balon	Stewart	Seiling	9:48	Det.	Baun	Crosscheck	5:55
	Det.	Howe	Brewer		17:29	N.Y.	Nevin	Hooking	8:32
	Det.	Libett	unassisted		19:05	Det.	Brewer	Interference	13:15
						Det.	Stemkowski	Tripping	16:02

goal while *playing* short-handed. This is rather unusual, but it was an unusual game! See if you can figure out how much time was left to be served in the penalty box when these two goals were scored.

Strategy: First add 2 minutes to the time of each penalty and check the chart to see whether that player's team scored a goal during his penalty. The first of these goals was during Nevin's penalty called at 8:32, when Balon scored for New York at 9:48.

Add 2 minutes to the time of Nevin's penalty:
$$\begin{array}{r} 8:32 \\ +2:00 \\ \hline 10:32. \end{array}$$

Then subtract the time of Balon's short-handed goal to see how much time Nevin had left to serve in his penalty:
$$\begin{array}{r} 10:32 \\ -\ 9:48 \\ \hline 0:44. \end{array}$$

Do the same thing to find Detroit's short-handed goal and to figure out how much time was left in Detroit's penalty when the goal was scored. Remember that you are working with minutes and seconds, so when you "borrow" in your subtraction, you must borrow 60 instead of 10.

Extra Points

If all the penalties had been served in full, there would have been 18 minutes of penalty time in this game. There were nine penalties of 2 minutes each; $9 \times 2 = 18$.

But as you probably know, when a short-handed team is scored against, the penalty automatically ends when the goal is scored even if the 2 minutes are not up. This is not true of major penalties, which are for 5 minutes. It is also not true when a short-handed team *scores* a goal; the penalty only ends when the short-handed team is scored *against*.

You found out in problems 4 and 7 that two goals were scored against short-handed teams in this game. See if you can figure out how much penalty time was actually served during the game. Remember that if the short-handed team scores, the penalty doesn't end; it only ends if the opposing team scores.

Strategy: Figure out how much time was served in each penalty by subtracting the time when the penalty was called from the time when the next goal was scored by the opposing team. Then add up all the penalty time served to find the total.

There is another way to do this. Since you know from problems 4 and 7 how much time was *not* served in the penalties, you can add these unserved times together and subtract them from the total penalty time imposed by the referees.

Hockey Sportsmath Answers

1.   242
    −237
        5 goals needed for Rangers to tie Montreal
        +1
        6 goals needed for Rangers to pass Montreal in total goals

2.   20:00   19:60
    −17:48   −17:48
                2:12 minutes left in first period when Egers scored

3. Gilbert: 1 goal
Ratelle: 1 assist
A. Brown: 3 assists
Egers: 2 goals
Nevin: 1 assist
Balon: 1 goal
Tkaczuk: 1 assist
Horton: 1 assist

Brown had 3 assists for 3 points, the most points scored by a player in this period.

4. Detroit penalty: 12:07
                + 2:00
Penalty would be over: 14:07

Penalty would be over: 14:07
N.Y. goal   −12:31
Time left in penalty: 1:36

5. 237   246
    +9   −242
    246 total goals for N.Y.   4 goals needed for
                                   Montreal   to   tie
                                   Rangers

        4
     + 1
        5 goals needed for Montreal to make the playoffs

OR   9 goals made by Rangers
       − 5 goals needed to tie Montreal
          4 goals needed by Montreal to tie Rangers

6. **Detroit**   **New York**

    Bergman: 1 goal   Gilbert: 2 goals
    Mahovlich: 1 goal   Egers: 2 goals
    Stemkowski: 1 goal   Balon: 3 goals
    Howe: 1 goal   Stewart: 2 goals,
    Libett: 1 goal,   1 assist
          1 assist   Ratelle: 2 assists
    Connelly: 1 assist   Nevin: 2 assists
    Delvecchio: 1 assist   Tkaczuk: 1 assist
    Brewer: 2 assists   Horton: 1 assist
    MacGregor: 1 assist   Kurtenbach: 2 assists
                                 A. Brown: 4 assists
                                 Park: 1 assist
                                 Seiling: 1 assist

    High scorers: 1st place: Brown—4 assists for 4 points
                  2nd place: Balon—3 goals for 3 points
                             Stewart—2 goals and 1 assist for
                             3 points

7. No goals were scored against a short-handed team in the 2nd and 3rd periods.

8.

N.Y. penalty:	8:32
	+ 2:00
penalty would be over:	10:32
	10:32
N.Y. goal:	−9:48
time left in penalty:	0:44
Detroit penalty:	16:02
	+ 2:00
penalty would be over:	18:02
	18:02
Detroit goal:	−17:29
time left in penalty:	0:33

Extra Points

1st period

N.Y. goal:	8:25
Det. penalty:	−6:26
time served:	1:59
N.Y. goal:	12:31
Det. penalty:	−12:07
time served:	0:24

2nd and 3rd periods

All penalties were served in full:	2:00
	× 7
	14:00

```
    14:00
     1:59
+    0:24
    16:23
```

OR

```
time not served in penalties       0:01
            in 1st period:       +1:36
                                  1:37
```

```
    18:00
−    1:37
    16:23
```

TENNIS SPORTSMATH

In the last few years tennis has become a very popular spectator sport. Most important tennis matches are now televised, and the attendance and prize money as well as the number of participating players has risen sharply. As in other sports, many numbers are used in scoring tennis matches and in making and breaking records. At the end of this chapter is a sample scorecard. You can make your own scorecards and follow your favorite players' progress.

Some of the most interesting numbers in tennis are the ones that show its tremendous rise in popularity. In this chapter you will discover ways to measure this rate of growth and to estimate what might be happening in tennis a few years from now if this rate of growth continues.

Tennis Facts

Number of players: In tennis there are never more than four people playing on a court at one time. In a singles game, two people play against one another; in a doubles game, one pair of players plays against another pair.

Scoring: In a tennis game a score of zero is called "love"; the first point is called "15," the second point "30," the third point "40," and the last point "game." (The first point may also be called "5.") If both sides reach 40, one side must score two points in a row to win the *game*. A score of 40–40 or any tie score after this point is called "deuce."

One side serves for a complete game, and the score of the side that is serving is announced first; for example, if the score is 15–40, the side that is not serving is ahead by two points.

In regular play, the first side to win six games wins the *set,* but again, the winning side must win by at least two games. So if the score is even at 5 games apiece, one side must win the next 2 games to win the set 7 games to 5 games.

A *match* generally consists of 3 sets for women, 5 sets for men. To win a match, one side must win 2 of 3 sets, or 3 of 5 sets.

In tournament play, the rules are different, and each tournament may have its own rules. A tiebreaker game may be played to determine the winner of a tied set, and the number of sets per match may vary.

Time: There is no time limit for a game, set, or match. Play continues until one side wins.

Court: The court is 78 feet long and 36 feet wide; it may have a grass, clay, or cement surface.

U.S. Open, 1974

The 1974 U.S. Open tennis tournament was held on the grass courts of the West Side Tennis Club in Forest Hills, New York. The women's singles semifinals pitted Chris Evert against Evonne Goolagong in one of the most dramatic and emotional matches ever played in women's tennis. The winner of the semifinal match would go on to the final round for the Women's U.S. Open Championship and $22,500 in prize money.

Women's tennis had begun to attract a wide audience in the

TENNIS COURT

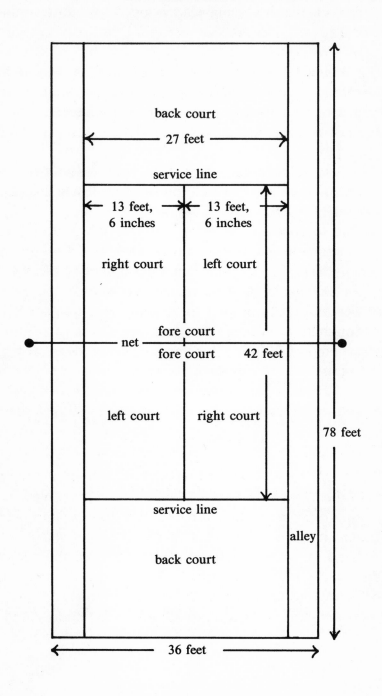

few years before 1974. Both the prize money for women and the number of women's events in the U.S. Open had increased dramatically.

1. In 1968 the women's first prize in the U.S. Open was $6,000. In 1974 Chris or Evonne would have a chance at a first prize of $22,500. Quite a difference! See if you can figure out the percentage of increase in the women's first prize from 1968 to 1974.

Strategy: To find the percentage of increase, divide the 1974 prize money figure by the figure for 1968. Carry your division to three decimal places and round off to the nearest hundredth: $22,500.000 \div 6,000 = ?$

Then write your answer as a percentage. Your answer will be a number that is larger than 1. Remember that 1.00 can be written as 100% (1.00 = 100/100 or 100%); so if your answer were 2.50 you would write it as 250%.

2. In the same period of time, the men's first prize money jumped from $14,000 in 1968 to $22,500 in 1974. Find the percent of increase in the men's first prize money.

Strategy: Find this percentage the same way you found the percentage of increase for the women's prize money—divide the figure for 1974 by the figure for 1968. Don't forget to work your answer to three decimal places and round off to the nearest hundredth. Then write the answer as a percentage.

3. Of course the women's and men's first prizes were not the only prizes awarded. The total amount of prize money awarded at the 1974 U.S. Open was $271,720. In 1968 the total prize money was $100,000. Figure out the percentage of increase of the total prize money.

Strategy: Again, to find this percentage, divide the 1974 figure by the 1968 figure. Be sure to keep all those zeroes straight!

4. Another way to tell how much more popular tennis has

become is to compare the total attendance at the 1968 and 1974 U.S. Opens. In 1974 the total attendance was 153,287; in 1968 it was only 97,294. What was the percentage of increase in attendance in those six years?

Strategy: Once again, divide the 1974 figure by the 1968 figure; work your answer to three decimal places and round to the nearest hundredth. Then write this number as a percentage.

The increase in attendance is not as startling as the percentage of increase in the total prize money. But don't forget that the 1974 tournament was televised, so that many more people than were actually there could see the matches.

In the women's semifinals in 1974, Chris Evert was favored to beat Evonne Goolagong. Nineteen-year-old Chris had won the hearts of American tennis fans three years earlier by reaching the semifinals at Forest Hills as an unseeded sixteen-year-old. Now she was seeded first in the tournament.

Seeding is the arrangement of the top-ranked players in a tournament, based on their performance in recent tournament play. The matches in the tournament are set up so that these top players, who are ranked in order of their chances to win, will not meet in the first few rounds of play. In the 1974 U.S. Open, when all the other women's singles matches were finished, only Chris Evert, Evonne Goolagong, Billie Jean King, and Julie Heldman remained unbeaten. King then won her semifinals match with Heldman. So the match between Chris and Evonne would determine who would play Billie Jean in the finals and have a shot at winning the U.S. Open.

Chris was under a lot of pressure to win. She was entering the match with an impressive string of 56 consecutive wins; she had not lost a single set during the tournament. Also, she was to marry tennis star Jimmy Connors in November and a great deal had already been written about their twin victories at Wimbledon in June of that year. If Chris won at Forest Hills, it would be another double victory.

Evonne, on the other hand, had been playing with the Pittsburgh Triangles of the World Team Tennis League, and had not been involved in as much tournament play as Chris had in 1974. In addition, she had been barred from participating in the 1974 French Open Championships because of her World Team Tennis play. However, Evonne had played in the important Wimbledon competition in the summer of 1974. She and Peggy Michel (a teammate of Evonne's on the Triangles) had won the women's doubles championship there, but Evonne had been upset in the quarterfinals of singles play. She was seeded fifth in the U.S. Open singles competition.

The match was set for Friday, September 6, and a crowd of 13,017 waited to see the clash of these two very different personalities. Evert was known as a "tennis player's tennis player." Writers and tennis fans referred to her as "cool," "stiff," an "icy shot-maker," and "unemotional." It was true that Chris rarely showed any emotion on the court and she seemed to plan each shot carefully. She had a powerful two-fisted backhand and impeccable ground strokes. But her biggest asset was her ability to concentrate on her game; at a crucial point she seemed able to bear down and pour out even more effort.

Evonne Goolagong, the free-spirited 23-year-old Australian star, was not as deliberate in her moves as Chris. But she had a deadly accurate shot and a strong one-handed backhand. With her graceful style, Evonne roamed the court more than Chris. Her fans claimed that her only weakness was her occasional loss of concentration. Sometimes Evonne played brilliant tennis and then suddenly began to miss easy points. These lapses of concentration were sometimes called Evonne's "walkabouts" (walkabout is an Australian word meaning a period of wandering in the bush, away from one's regular work).

With Evert favored to win, the semifinals match began; the winner would have to take two of the three sets.

Surprisingly, the first set took just fifteen minutes. Evonne flawlessly batted winning shots from all over the court and won the first six games in a convincing victory that made her fifth seeding look ridiculous. Chris didn't win a single game in the set. She made unusual mistakes and her playing was erratic—not what the fans expected from "Miss Cool."

A drizzle began during the second set. Goolagong was ahead 4 games to 2 on superb shots and it looked as if she would win a fifth. But Chris struck back with an impressive high looping shot to the back of the court which Evonne couldn't return, and the game score was 4 to 3.

Then the rains really came down. Play became dangerous as the players slid on the grass surface, and the match was halted. For three and a half hours the fans, judges, and players waited for the rain to stop, but the match was finally cancelled for the day. The rain continued for two and a half days.

It was difficult for both players to have the match delayed so long. Evonne had been playing brilliant tennis and the long layoff might slow down her momentum. Chris had a long time to think about her mistakes, but she also had time to regain her confidence and determination.

5. While waiting for the rain to stop, the officials of the U.S. Open were probably doing some sportsmath of their own. Not only had the prize money and attendance increased dramatically in the last few years, but the number of entries had also increased. (Since some players are entered in more than one event, the number of entries is larger than the number of players in the tournament.)

In 1968 the total number of entries was 280 in 5 events. By 1974 the total number of entries had increased to 426 in 10 events. It is clear that the number of events had doubled, or

U.S. OPEN

Number of entries	1974		1968	
Women's singles	64		64	
Women's doubles	64		32	
Mixed doubles (64 men and women)	32	women	0	
Junior girls	16		0	
Total women's entries	—		—	
Total men's entries	—		—	
Total number of entries	426	(10 events)	280	(5 events)

increased by 200%. But the number of entries had not doubled. By what percentage did the number of entries increase?

Strategy: Divide the total number of entries in 1974 by the total for 1968. Work your answer to three decimal places and round it to the nearest hundredth. Then write this number as a percentage.

6. Some of the women's events in 1974 were not played in the 1968 U.S. Open. Use the chart to find the total number of women's entries for 1974 and 1968. By what percentage has the number of entries in women's events at the Open increased?

Strategy: Add the women's entries in 1974 and in 1968 to find the total number of women's entries for each year. Then divide the 1974 total by the total for 1968. Remember to work your answer to three decimal places and round it to the nearest hundredth; then write the answer as a percentage.

7. Although the chart doesn't give the breakdown of the men's entries, you can find the men's total entries for each year and then find the percentage of increase in men's entries. Would you guess that it is a larger or smaller increase than the women's?

Strategy: First subtract the women's total entries for 1974 from

Evonne Goolagong playing hard at Wimbledon in 1974, preparing for her appearance in the U.S. Open.

United Press International Photo

the total number of entries for that year to find the men's total. Find the 1968 men's total the same way. Then use long division to find the percentage of increase in men's entries, working the problem the same way you did the women's.

There was a great deal of suspense as Chris and Evonne got ready to resume the match. Evonne served well and won the game, which put her ahead 5 games to 3 in the set. She needed only one more game to win the set. With the win of this second set, she would win the match and the semifinals.

Chris was serving and Evonne was leading 15–40. Only one more point to win the match! But Chris fought to hold her serve and she won the game. The score of the second set was now 5 games to 4.

In the next game, with Evonne serving, the two struggled for points. Evonne could still win the match by winning this game. Twice Evonne was one point from winning but was stopped by Chris's determination. Then, on a disputed Goolagong shot, with Chris one point from winning the game, a lineswoman called a ball "in" that Chris thought had gone out. After some heated discussion, the lineswoman asked the umpire to settle the dispute. The umpire overruled the lineswoman and called the ball out. The point was Chris's and the game score became 5 all!

Each player won another game and the score was 6 to 6. This called for a special rule: a 9-point tiebreaker game would be played to determine the winner of the second set. Each player was to take two turns serving until one player scored 5 points. The first player to reach 5 points would win the tiebreaker game and the second set. Once again, if Evonne could win, she would win the match.

The score in the tiebreaker was even at 3–3 when suddenly Evonne made a forehand error. Then Chris rallied with deadly strokes to make the fifth point. Evert had fought back to win the tiebreaker game and the second set. Now the players had one set apiece, and a third set would be played to decide the winner of the match. The crowd was ecstatic. Even though Chris was the favorite, she had never beaten Evonne on grass courts before. Surely this was the turning point. Chris was finally getting her game together.

In the third set, Evonne jumped to a 3-game lead. But Chris fought back and won 2 games with dazzling shots. Goolagong won the next game to make the score 4 to 2. Evert again came back to make it 4–3. Goolagong bore down and pulled away to 5–3. Again, Evonne needed just one more game to win the match.

Chris refused to give up; she battled to return Evonne's powerful serve. Finally, Evonne hit a beautiful overhead shot to come within one point of winning the game. On a beautiful backhand volley, she smacked home the winning shot and took the match! Chris Evert had been beaten after 56 straight wins.

The crowd greeted Evonne and Chris with a standing ovation. Evonne had beaten Chris in a hard-fought and exciting match. Chris had played brilliantly, chasing shots all over the court, but Evonne had shown that she could concentrate when she had to.

And now it was off to the finals for Evonne Goolagong and another chance next year for Chris Evert in the U.S. Open.

8. Since the men's and women's first prize money are the same now at Forest Hills, it is unlikely that they will increase at different rates. But if tennis grows in popularity in the next six-year period the way it did from 1968 to 1974, what would the total prize money be in 1980?

Strategy: From problem 3 on page 83, you already know the rate of increase in total prize money from 1968 to 1974. Write this percentage in decimal form again, the way it was when you

Chris Evert (at right) congratulates Evonne Goolagong after Evonne
won their semifinal match at Forest Hills in September, 1974.
United Press International Photo

worked the long division problem and rounded your answer to
the nearest hundredth. Then multiply this percent, now written
as a decimal, by the amount of the total prize money in 1974.

TENNIS SCORECARD

Set No. *1*

Game No.	server	points										Game Score Goolagong	Evert
1	G	15	15	30	30	40	X					1	0
2												2	0
3												3	0
4												4	0
5												5	0
6												6	0
7													
8													
9													
10													

This sample scorecard shows the first set of the Evert-Goolagong match. The score has only been filled in for the first game.

This will tell you the amount of the total prize money in 1980 if it continues to increase at the same rate.

Match Point

You can use the same method to figure out the total number of entries and the total attendance for 1980. But remember, if you keep these numbers tucked away in a drawer to see whether they come true, there is a limit to the seating capacity and to the number of players that can be accomodated, even if there is no limit to the prize money that could be awarded.

Strategy: Do these projections the same way you did the one for the prize money: multiply the figure for 1974 by the percentage of increase from 1968 to 1974. Remember to keep your decimal points in place.

Tennis Sportsmath Answers

1.
```
            3.750
6,000 | 22,500.000
```
3.750 rounded off and written as a percentage is 375%. The women's first prize money increased by 375% from 1968 to 1974.

2.
```
             1.607
14,000 | 22,500.000
```
The men's first prize money increased by 161% from 1968 to 1974.

3.
```
              2.717
100,000 | 271,720.000
```
The total prize money for the U.S. Open increased by 272% from 1968 to 1974.

4.
```
             1.575
97,294 | 153,287.000
```
The total attendance at the U.S. Open increased by 158% from 1968 to 1974.

5.
```
          1.521
280 | 426.000
```
The total number of entries in the U.S. Open increased by 152% from 1968 to 1974.

6.
```
  64        64
  64        32
  32         0
+ 16       + 0                1.833
 176        96        96 | 176.000
```
The number of women's entries in the U.S. Open increased by 183% from 1968 to 1974.

7.
```
 426       280
-176       - 96                1.358
 250       184        184 | 250.000
```
The number of men's entries in the U.S. Open increased by 136% from 1968 to 1974.

8. $271,720.00
        $\times$ 2.72
$739,078.4000
If the amount of prize money increased at the same rate, there would be $739,078.40 in total prize money at the U.S. Open in 1980.

Match Point
    153,287
    $\times$ 1.58
242,193.46
If total attendance increased at the same rate, there would be 242,193 spectators at the 1980 U.S. Open.
    426
$\times$1.52
647.52
If entries increased at the same rate, there would be 648 entries in the 1980 U.S. Open.

INDEX

95